HISTORY®
UNBOXED

# MYSTERIES
## OF THE SHARK HUNTERS

## THE JOMON
## OF ANCIENT JAPAN

By Elizabeth Hauris
Illustrations by Matthew Maley

The Jomon lived in the Stone Age.
What does this mean?
Did they live in caves?
Did they hunt dinosaurs?
Did they use lumpy rock tools?
No!
The Stone Age means stone was
used to make tools.

The Jomon lived in houses.

These houses were dug into the ground.

The walls and floor were earth.

The roof was woven of branches and grasses.

Inside the house was warm and safe.

The wind could not get in.

The earth walls held the heat from a cozy fire.

The roof kept the family dry.

The Jomon hunted many animals.
Big animals.
Fierce animals.
Tasty animals.
But not dinosaurs.
Dinosaurs died a long, long time
before people walked the earth

What animals did the Jomon see?
They collected shellfish to eat,
like mussels, oysters, and clams.
They hunted little animals,
like rabbits and birds.
But they also hunted BIG animals,
like boars, bears, sharks, and whales!

The Jomon made wonderful hunting tools.
They made a harpoon to hunt at sea.
They made the harpoon from stone and wood.
It worked so well that people today,
with modern tools and metal,
have not been able to make a harpoon
that is better for hunting.

There was another animal
that the Jomon loved,
but not to eat!
It was one of the first times in the world
that people had an animal best friend
with soft fur
and a wagging tail
and a loud bark.
Do you know what animal made friends with the Jomon?

Dogs!
The Jomon were some of the first people
to raise dogs
and use them for hunting
and scratch behind their ears.
Do you have a dog
you like to play with?
Thank the Jomon!

The Jomon ate their veggies,
but they did not have gardens.
They walked around the forest
and the beach
and the fields
and they gathered tasty things to eat.
Yummy chestnuts.
Chewy acorns.
Juicy berries.
Fresh greens.
Slippery seaweed.
And they had a special way
to get everything ready to eat

The Jomon made cooking pots.
They dug clay from the ground
and shaped it with their hands.
They dried it out
and baked it in the fire
so the pot could hold water.

What a great idea!
Now they could make soup!
Now they could cook nuts, grains, and meat
until everything was soft and yummy.
This made the food easier to digest.
This meant the Jomon could grow stronger
and have more energy
to make beautiful things.

The Jomon made art.
They wove baskets out of branches and vines and grass.
They shaped stone and clay into tiny people and animals.
They pressed designs into their clay pots.
This is why the Jomon are called The Rope People.
They decorated their clay pots with rope.
They took pieces of rope
and pressed them into the soft clay,
leaving behind a pretty design

The Jomon did not leave us writing.
No one in the world knew how to write yet!
They did not leave us stories.
They lived too long ago for anyone to remember
what they might have said.
But they did leave us art.
They left us tools.
And they left clues about how they lived
in unusual places.

One of the ways we know about the Jomon is from poop!
The Jomon had a place to use the bathroom.
They dug pits in the ground
and used the pits as their toilet.
This kept the village clean.
They even trained their dogs to use the pit toilet!
Then they would throw in sea shells.

Why?
The sea shells are made of calcium.
Calcium changes the poop
so it does not rot.
And it does not make the ground dirty.
And it does not make the water dirty.
And it does not make people sick in the village.
Everything stayed cleaner.
And because the Jomon did this,
archeologists could find their poop
fourteen thousand years later!
And learn about what they ate
and how they lived.

The Jomon lived fourteen thousand years ago
in the Stone Age
where the country of Japan now stands
How long ago was fourteen thousand years?

It can be hard to imagine.
The United States is two hundred and fifty years old.
Imagine from the beginning of America to now,
then imagine that fifty six times!

The Jomon lived so long ago
we do not even know their name.
We call them "Jomon"
which means "Rope People"
because of the art they left behind.

www.ingramcontent.com/pod-product-compliance
Lightning Source LLC
Chambersburg PA
CBHW051651120626
46551CB00015B/2312